Prayers and Poems

–

Dissolving the Ego in the Divine

Yogani

From The AYP Enlightenment Series

Copyright © 2024 by AYP Publishing

All rights reserved.

Advanced Yoga Practices (AYP)

For ordering information go to:

www.advancedyogapractices.com

ISBN 978-1-938594-72-4 (Hardcover)
ISBN 978-1-938594-70-0 (Paperback)
ISBN 978-1-938594-71-7 (eBook)

This is for you who seek union with the Inner Divine…

Introduction

My path started when I was an adventurous child, and likely long before that, though I did not recognize it until stumbling into a daily meditation practice in the early 1970s, which has been going ever since. This book is to shed some light on the "middle years" of my path, sharing prayers and poems written in the 1980s, about 15 years after beginning meditation, and about 15 years before starting to write the Advanced Yoga Practices (AYP) lessons in the early 2000s, which has gone on for another 20 years since then.

This is a snapshot of what life was like for a busy householder and career person more than a decade into a daily meditation practice. By then, multiple additions to practice had been implemented, with the establishment of abiding inner silence (the witness) and kundalini awakening, all eventually documented, expanded on and refined in the AYP writings to assist a wide range of practitioners.

But let's go back for a minute. I was born in New York City in 1947 to Dutch immigrant parents, the oldest of three siblings, grew up in suburban New Jersey, went to a technology university in Atlanta, Georgia, married in 1970, moved to Florida where we raised three children who now have families of their own, and my wife and I are now "retired" in a relatively quiet life with family close by. A pretty ordinary life for the most part, with plenty of struggles along the way. There has been nothing special about me, except daily spiritual practices over the years, which anyone can do with a dedicated discipline.

My public writing has always been about attempting to help seekers develop and maintain an effective and safe spiritual practice. My private writing, mostly long ago, has been about my path. This book shares previously private writings on what was occurring during the middle stage of spiritual development, involving the active (desperate!) surrender of the ego to the divine (blissful inner silence), driven by the challenges of egoistical living in the material world. The hope is that it will provide some inspiration for others who find themselves in similar circumstances on their path. With intense bhakti (devotion) and established abiding inner silence (witness), a merging to oneness with the divine (non-duality) and an outpouring of divine love will happen. It is a liberating experience, with benefits reaching far beyond the individual practitioner.

So, with that background, let's get into it. The first thing in here is a letter written in the late 1980s to a fellow practitioner, detailing where I was in practices and experiences at the time, the worldly struggles I was dealing with that were driving increasing bhakti/devotion, and early thoughts about "publishing." It was a messy time. As they say, "Desperate times call for desperate measures," and that is what was going on then. Little did I know that, much later, openings occurring then would lead to the massive AYP outpouring. The phrase, "Be careful what you wish for" comes to mind. Absolutely no regrets on that. Everything has happened as it should.

Over time, I opened fully to the flow from within, leading to the publication of *The Secrets of Wilder* novel, the nearly 1000 AYP online lessons, and more than a dozen books on practice. All of that had little to do with me. It came from within and had to do with everyone else. But back in the 1980s, it was still mostly about me. So pardon the old self-indulgent writings in this book, which were a turning point on my path. You can see a progression in the prayers and poems as my experience evolved during that transformative time. If it helps you on your path, great. If not, let it go. If it isn't a help now, maybe it will be later, adapted for your particular needs. Or perhaps you have been through this kind of middle stage experience already, and can relate to the struggles of inner awakening documented here. It is offered with love.

As always, the guru is in you.

Yogani
2024

Contents

1. Letter to a Fellow Practitioner (1988) 1
2. Turning Point..4
3. Role of Worldly Difficulties...............................5
4. Assessing the Mind...6
5. Recognition of Sacrifice 7
6. For Others...8
7. This Life 9
8. Eternal Consciousness 9
9. World vs. Transcendence 10
10. Service 10
11. Adversity 11
12. He, She, or It?...11
13. Conditions...12
14. To the Lord 12
15. My Human Weaknesses 13
16. Don't Let Me Stray..13
17. Teaching the Child 14
18. City of God..15
19. Spectacle 15
20. On Variations...16
21. Sacred Seed 16
22. All I Have to Give 17
23. What Will Happen? 17
24. Holy Spirit 18
25. Pursuit..18
26. Worm and Butterfly.......................................18
27. I am All..19
28. Impatience 20
29. Desperate 20
30. The Laughter 20
31. Dialog on THAT..21
32. Lost 22
33. Rise!...22

34. Petition for Union 23
35. Waiting for the Goddess 23
36. Prayer to the Goddess 24
37. Sweet Lady 25
38. In This Life 25
39. Fever Pitch 26
40. Judging a Civilization 26
41. Life in the Shadows 27
42. Where is Your Form? 27
43. Clogged 28
44. Single Eye 28
45. Making Love 29
46. God 29
47. Love 30
48. More Love 30
49. Fear 31
50. The World as Excrement 31
51. Living in Two Worlds 32
52. Disciplines 32
53. Fearing Death 33
54. On Writing Books 33
55. Letting Go 34
56. Living in Mud 35
57. My Self-Contained Religion 36
58. What is Enlightenment? 37
59. Desire 37
60. All I Think About 38
61. Materialism 39
62. Forces of Darkness 39
63. How Can I Get Upset? 40
64. Illusion 40
65. Longing for the Truth 40
66. There is Only One 41
67. Truth Within 42
68. Life is a Hangnail 43

69. Useless World..43
70. What Have I Done? 44
71. The Rope 45
72. No Wisdom Today 45
73. On Pain 46
74. God Realization 46
75. The Way I Am..47
76. The Great Beyond..48
77. To Another...49
78. The Witness 50
79. The Word God...50
80. Practice 51
81. Lady of Light...52
82. Dinosaurs...53
83. Yogi Bob 54
84. Book Group 54
85. The Wave and the Sea 54
86. Darkness and Light..55
87. Soma..56
88. He Not Seen...57
89. Mammon..57
90. Beyond the Birds and Bees..............................58
91. Inner Bright 60
92. The Old Picture Show 61
93. Embrace of the Goddess 61
94. What is This Fear?...62
95. Madness...63
96. Reincarnation...64
97. Third Person 64
98. Where Are You Going?....................................65
99. Love and Longing..66
100. Simplicity 66
101. USA 67
102. Mind 68
103. Death..68

104. Brother 69
105. Sister 70
106. The Master 71
107. Path of Love 71
108. Surrender 72
109. Alone? 73
110. Helpless 74
111. The Upper Room 75
112. Sunday Play 76
113. The Seed 77
114. Experiences and God 77
115. Ego Devils 78
116. A Turn in Me 79
117. Heart Flower 80
118. Free Will 80
119. Light 81
120. Crazy Driver 82
121. The Rise of Experience 83
122. Letting it Go 83
123. A Billion Hearts 84
124. Celibacy 84
125. No Escape 85
126. Lover in the Heart 86
127. Believe Me 87
128. The Gift 87
129. No Place to Hide 88
130. My Heart 89
131. Nectar 89
132. Chinese Saying 90
133. To My Sons 91
134. Heart Wails 92
135. He is Everywhere 93
136. Challenge 93
137. What Could I Offer? 94
138. Simple Argument 94

139. On Business 95
140. Real vs. Unreal 95
141. How Strong Can It Be? 96
142. Another World 97
143. Misunderstood 98
144. Ocean of Bliss..98
145. Perspective on Experience 99
146. Vibrations and Flames 99
147. Ecstasy Alert..100
148. Overrated 101
149. Shakti Effect 101
150. Breath 101
151. Death of the American Child..........................102
152. Dissolved 103
153. Fame 103
154. Karma 104
155. Thorns and Mud 104
156. Waterford Princess 105
157. Simple Wisdom 106
158. Veil of Words 107
159. Marshmallow Mother 108
160. "I" 108
161. Half Lit Kit 109
162. I Want My Halo Back 109
163. Finger Switch Mitch 110
164. There is a Bigness 110
165. Listen to the Love 111
166. No Cross Have I 112
167. The Seer 113
168. Being Me 113
169. Eternity 114

Further Reading and Support 117

Dissolving the Ego –   xi

1. Letter to a Fellow Practitioner (1988)

Dear John,

Here are several years' worth of writing. There is plenty more prior to this, but this is enough for now.

My attempts at poetry have only been in the past year. Prior to that is has been mostly prayers, which have been an important part of my path. There are hundreds of them, sometimes morphing into poems. I have picked out some that might offer a message, and even these may not be of much interest to most people.

Along with the prayers and poems, I have been keeping a detailed record of my experiences, yoga practices, etc. for many years. There is enough of that to write a big book. Maybe it will all come out after I am dead. Much of it is controversial, given the secrecy surrounding spiritual practices, and the condemnation of anyone violating the "code of silence."

Periodically I get the urge to publish something along spiritual lines. There is even a prayer in here about that (#54). I am feeling some comfort about trying this someday with the prayers and poems. What do you think? The poems are coming pretty quickly now as my experiences unfold. We'll see.

1985 is where any published writing should start, because this is when I went through a major turning point toward surrender after about 6 or 7 years of an ego-based "God supporting my business career" philosophy. It was truly nonsense, and repeated warnings were ignored by me in my greed-driven endeavors. Finally in 1984-85, after starting my own business, it became apparent that I would not survive on an ego-based strategy. No way it could happen. Keep in mind that this was after nearly 15 years of meditation, including substantial additional practices picked up along the way, so my practice routine includes pretty much the whole bit. Expecting divine support in my business goes to show you what a stubborn child the ego is.

No doubt the most difficult task on the spiritual path is the surrender of the ego in stillness. Perhaps it is the only task, for once this is accomplished, everything else comes. Teachings I am familiar with do not even discuss "surrender" until one is established in 24/7 witness consciousness. At this point, for me, surrender is an attractive alternative for the ego because the divine begins to be perceived as more fulfilling than the world. The ego (mind) then can choose surrender more easily. Prior to this point, surrender is a threat to the ego and it has a million defenses against the mere idea of surrender. Meditation undermines the ego, in a manner of speaking, because it reveals the Self behind it all. As the silent Self becomes more clear and real as subject, the ego becomes less real along with everything else in the objective illusory world. The ego is more easily given up once it is seen as an illusory object, which can only be done with the silent Self established. Prior to this, the ego sees itself as the subject!

I also went back over some of my notes from the 1970s. From the early 70s, when meditation started, until around 1979, I was on a strong spiritual bent. This was when I did a lot of spiritual reading, and my journal entries are quite purposeful in terms of "the divine quest." There are attempts at devotion during that time, but ego spills out all over it, and worldly pursuits are most often center stage, supporting a growing family, with spiritual power in a supporting role. It is somewhat frightening to review that period and the "fall" I experienced from a mental standpoint from the late 1970s until the mid-1980s. My daily practice of meditation during the disappointments of the world finally cleared things up to where I was able to embark on the adventure alluded to in the following prayers and poems. What is frightening is the possibility of another fall. Spiritually, it was like the great depression.

There are some obvious differences now. Then (1970s), I was inspired by the logic of philosophy, and the inner silence I was experiencing through regular practice and periodic retreats. Now, I still have the philosophy, the steady inner silent witness, plus my "electric light show" (kundalini awakening). But, you know, there is still the chance of a fall. I'm not even sure I have risen very high to fall from. The prayers and poems here are not the product of an enlightened person. They are the product of one who is doubting while immersed in advanced experiences. Whether or not I can pass through to the other side of this is still an unknown. Fixations on name and fame, wealth, power, and even sexual obsessions could lead to a fall in a hurry. Ramakrishna called worldly pursuits, "women and gold."

I am truly on the razor's edge, crossing a giant abyss. I feel somewhat safe right now because I have a monastery type of existence, really. I have deliberately nailed down my worldly life into a series of ruts. I hardly have to think about it. It's quite boring at times, but I am free to concentrate on my spiritual development, which currently requires a great deal of mental and physical energy.

Any major extended upset in this routine would upset a delicate balance. I fear this greatly. This fear is okay, in fact beneficial. Bhakti training says all emotions are directed toward God. Fear of losing or not merging with the divine within is productive. It brings help. So I cultivate this fear. You can do the same with your anger, John. When you are angry, you can redirect it to being frustrated that you have not merged with the divine within, and pointing that anger toward the inner divine will bring help.

I have collated and shared these prayers and poems because I want to understand the lessons of my past, and move forward as quickly as possible into an awakened future. Perhaps the writings can be helpful to you in reviewing your priorities for spiritual growth. Transcendence is the key, then surrender of the ego to the transcendent divine, in that order.

Best wishes on your path…

2. Turning Point

My Lord,
My God,

You are the destination in me.
Much of the time my vision is clouded by
attachments to this world and this body.
But, still, I know You are the destination in me.

Lord,

And eventually I will reach the destination.
And You and I will be One.
Because I know there is no other but You.
And because there is no other, then
I must be Your expression even now.
Thy will be done!

Dear God,

How important it is to live Your reality.
There is no other.
From the silent depths to the multitude of forms,
It is all You!
I shall live in union with Your divine nature.

3. Role of Worldly Difficulties

God,
Father,

You have placed me in a difficult situation,
But the benefit is now apparent.
You have turned my greed for success into a hunger for You.
For Thou art the only reality.
And so, I have turned to You
Deep within myself, and everywhere around.
May I be constantly bathed in Your presence.
May I never forget, or be led astray from You.
Thy will be done!

My Lord,

In my heart, I know that all
Will be added to me by Your grace.
For You are the source of all things.
May I use the things of this world
To further Your purpose.
And may I find You smiling in all things
I encounter in your creation.

God,

May I find eternal union in You.
May my will be Your will, always.
May I act freely to express Your will
In Your creation.
May I be the perfect expression of You.

My Love,
My God,

To write these words opens the doors.
Swing them wide!
Let Thy Being leap forth to my senses and consciousness.
It is time for You to stream into my life,
Never to recede again.
Make me Your perfect instrument.
Thy will be done!

Dear God,

Let us break down the barriers.
Let us be together as one.
Let my consciousness be Yours.
The truth is so plain.
Let me master the temptations which lead astray,
And find eternal union in You.

4. Assessing the Mind

My God,

Thy will be done

My Lord,

Let Your waves of bliss rise through my devotion to You.
I must say, when You rise in me, it is a bit muddy.
It is my lack of purification which brings the mud.

Let the mud be washed away so You will shine pure through my nature.
May my outer expression be your expression of the eternal reality.

God,

I need wisdom to discern and sort through the desires rising in me,
So I may choose to act on those serving You alone.
My small ego is so easily swayed to attach to many of these desires which rise.
May I choose correctly so my ego will be absorbed in Your divine consciousness,
And we shall be One!

5. Recognition of Sacrifice

Dear God,

With love for You I ask one thing.
Bring me close to You so I may reflect Your will in this world.

Lord,

I know this is not always pleasant for my small ego,
Which still needs much training from You.
I accept the cup whether it brings pleasure or pain.

God,

Let the pain be mine, not my loved ones'.
They are the sweetest among Your children.
Bring them peace and happiness.
As for me, I am prepared to carry the burden.
I am Yours.

My Lord,

If pain be what You have for me, I'll take it.
But I much prefer Your blissful presence,
Your divine vision, and Your all-consuming power.
Make me worthy of Thee.

6. For Others

Dearest Father in Heaven,

Many of Your children are lost and set in their ways.
I ask Your illumination for them.

Oh Lord,

Your Son the Christ Jesus said it all.
He taught us we are all Your children.
He called himself the Son.
He said, "I and my Father are One."

Oh God,

We, Your children, are One with our Father also.
This Your children will know in due time,
As we become less confused,
And less set in our ways.

7. This Life

Dear God,
My Father,

I cannot count the times I have lived
Certainly not enough times for Thee
I cannot count the times I've seen
Heaven…
Or Hell…
Nor can I tell if I am ready to finish the game
And come home to You
But this is what I want
To come home to You
And get us off this wheel

8. Eternal Consciousness

Every moment is but a blip
Upon the screen of
My eternal consciousness

9. World vs. Transcendence

This world is ups and downs
So many pleasures and pains
Forever riding the joys and sorrows
And losses and gains abounding
Where is the peace in all of this?
Where is That which transcends birth and death?
The peace is in That which is beyond the world
That which dwells within my innermost heart
That which has witnessed all births and deaths
That which is the eternal God

10. Service

Lord,

You have kept me very busy
Running to and fro
And little has come of it
But what does it matter?
I am in Your service
These big storms which rage all around
Cannot separate me from You
My love is growing
And I know that You will feed me
And my loved ones
So what does it matter?
I am in Your service

God,

But you know there is more
That I can do for You
Yet, it has not been time

For I have not been moved to do it
I am not ready yet
My depth must be greater
My love deeper
My steadfastness stronger
Then I can do it
Then I can make a good show for You
And fulfill Your purpose for me
I pray for Your blessing in this

11. Adversity

Adversity is one of God's greatest blessings
Sooner or later, it will bring us home to Him

12. He, She, or It?

The mystery of God defies the greatest theologians
Is He One?
Or is He many?
Is He a She, or an It?
Which is it?
Ah!
But He is!
He is!
And Ah!
She is!
She is!
And Ah again!
It is!
It truly is!
God responds to our devotion

No question about it
And when we transcend
We find God as our own inner Self
What else matters?
The mystery is solved!

13. Conditions

Lord of my life,
Thee whom I seek to realize,

Forgive me, for my love for You has conditions
I have judged Thy Grace by material ends in my life
You have told me so many times this is not the way
For Your kingdom is not of this transitory world
Oh how I wail for Thee in my heart!
Free me by Thy Grace from delusion that holds me!
I know that You hear my every plea
For You live within my heart
So hear this call to Thee
Free me!

14. To the Lord

Lord in my heart,

The thought of Thee gives me a thrill
Yet my restless mind wanders still
By Thy Grace only can I keep Thee near
And through Thee comes the loss of fear
In my heart Thy alter shines
And fills me with Thy light divine

15. My Human Weaknesses

Lord,

I have human desires, but I surely want You
I admit it
I have desires for women, wealth and power
And for possessions and experiences
Earthly and Divine.
It is my greatest desire to want You most
And to bring all my desires in tune with Your will
And how is this to be done?
By offering all my actions and achievements to You
If something good comes, I should give it to You
For it is not mine
If something bad comes, that is Yours also
For what is here that can give me eternal joy?
Why should I claim that which is unreal?
Yet, I appear to live here in the world
And I have these desires
So let them go on
Let them be fulfilled if it be Your will
Let my fulfillment be Yours
And may we enjoy the wonders of Your creation
Together

16. Don't Let Me Stray

Lord,

I have the clarity to fulfill Thy divine will
Within this city of Yours - this body
Much is to be done
I have a general idea of things to come

If there is to be pain
Let it be for the proper result
Let me not stray down the dark path
When there is bliss, let me stay clear
On thy inner mission
And complete the process fully
And most important of all
Let me not wander in my love for Thee
For I am Thy child
And long for Thy full presence
Here in this city of Thine

17. Teaching the Child

Oh Lord,

Like a little child you are teaching me
The facts of Divine Life
Out of the recesses of my soul it comes
The most precious wisdom of the ages
For certainly what can be more blissful
Than to experience the glory of
Thy Divine Romance
And yet, my experience is only a faint glimmer
Of the beginning of Your rise in me
How will I contain Thy full glory?
How will I ever be able to give attention
To the mundane things of this earth?
Ah, but we are going to do it
We are going to do it all this time
This body is ready
This soul is ready
Ready to join Thee in eternal bliss

18. City of God

Lord,

Thy name is Truth
I seek Thy Truth in total

Thy city is this body
Thy nature is heat and fire
Thy nature is pleasure and bliss
Burn this ego in Thy fire!
Take my love
For I give myself to Thee
Consume the sacred seed
And rise to the highest planes of bliss

Take me into Thy arms
Protect me, nurture me, love me
For I am Thy son and Thy lover
You are my Father, my Mother, and my Lover
By all means shall our union be completed
My love is safe with Thee
And Thy love is safe with me

19. Spectacle

Lord,

These experiences are a spectacle to my awareness
Energy pulsating up and down my spine
Pleasure everywhere
But this is not it
Not the purpose
For I want union with Thee

My love for Thee is eternal
As I know Thy love is eternal for me
Together we are lost in love
My desire for Thee is unbearable
It cannot bear to be unfulfilled
This emptiness must be filled
With Thy Grace

20. On Variations

If you don't like it, accept it
For like and dislike are born of the ego
And he/it is not a factor anymore
Pleasure, pain, gain, loss, joy, sorrow…
All of these are but variations in the One
Be the One
And let the variations be what they may
There is nothing to be had in them

21. Sacred Seed

Lord,

Thy blessed seed rises in me
Gathered from Thy sacred lowland fields
And carried by effort to the mountain top
By what paths do Thee bring this Bliss?
I see Thee hurrying up by all paths
And on the mountain top I wait in silence
For Thy seed is brought up
To bring forth the divine flower
That drips divine nectar into the whole world

22. All I Have to Give

Lord,

What can I give to Thee?
All this is Thine alone already
There is only one thing I can give to Thee
What Thou hast given me in the beginning
My separateness
My separateness is all I have to give
Myself is all I have to give
The thought of two is all I have to give
I give to Thee the thought of two
I give to Thee my separateness, myself
This is all I have to give
And I give it freely

23. What Will Happen?

Lord,

You are the destination in me
Is it possible to achieve this
While in the world?
So many distractions
Responsibilities and diversions
Yet, this soul is committed
To Thy glory
What will happen?

24. Holy Spirit

Holy Spirit, enter into Thy sacred channel!
Rise up to Thy celestial abode!
Thrill Thy entire creation!
Join with Thy mate, the Holy Father!
And bring forth Thy child the Christ!

25. Pursuit

Oh Lord, my Love
I will pursue Thee
Beyond the bounds
Of time and space!

26. Worm and Butterfly

Oh Lord,

I am but a worm
Creeping in the dirt
Living on the grubs
And carcasses of the world
But I shall enter Thy silver cocoon
And soon emerge
As Your Celestial Butterfly
Sipping divine nectar
From every sweet flower
In Thy garden
It is for this I was born
But a worm

27. I am All

I am All
I look into the eyes of another
And see my own Self
How can I be shy
Looking at my Self?
How can I fear anything
When all are aspects of my own Self?
So many faces have I
All so different
Yet all the same
I am the light
Shining out in all
Enjoy the love
That is everywhere
The unity of it all

What of pleasure and pain?
Joy and sorrow?
Gain and loss?
These are the reminders
Of what is not
They are fleeting
And press the issue
Of realizing the Self in all

After all
There are nothing but
Opportunities in the world
To see the Self
It lurks in all that is perceived
Take joy in It
Because all is
Thy own Self

28. Impatience

Oh, my Sweet Lord
When will I see You?
When will I feel Your Loving Embrace?
When will I taste Your Sweet Nectar?
When will I smell Your Divine Scent?
When will I hear Your Celestial Melodies?
I long for You!
You must come to me soon!
Or I will surely die!

29. Desperate

Lord, You know I want you
Completely
You are none but
My silent Self
Eternal Bliss Consciousness
You are the destination in me
And I am desperate
For realization of You

30. The Laughter

Laughter
The laughter of release
Like it's all a silly joke
This is what I hear
In deep meditation now
The laughter of the sages
Telling me it is okay

It is silly
To worry about this transient life
For there is eternal life in joy
Just beyond the darkness
Of this world
So laugh
Laugh out loud
What a relief
There is no death
Only awakening
To the hilarity of eternity

31. Dialog on THAT

I are That!
And what is That?
That is what I are!
What?!
I are everything!
What?
Everything!
Come on!
Honest!
How you know dis?
I see It
I feel It
I am It
Me too?
Yep, you too
Oh
Love You
Aw gee!
You are That!
See?
Yep

32. Lost

Lord,

You are so tender inside me
Spreading loving arms all around
Kissing the face of the entire world
With Your Love so sweet
Melting hearts with a glance
How can I put words
To this presence of God?
I cannot describe it
I can only be lost
In these waves of bliss
Swallowed up in the ecstasy
Of Love everywhere
Lord, I am yours in complete surrender
And you are mine
We are One

33. Rise!

Oh Mother!
Oh Holy Ghost!
Come up Your channel clear!
Come up and meet Your Husband!
Take Him!
For He waits for you
In His eternal silence!
He is the Father of all!
And He awaits His reunion
With You Oh Mother!
Join Him in ecstatic union!

Dissolve the separation between you!
And become One!
Rise!
Become One!

34. Petition for Union

Dear Lord,
My God,
My Self,

Make this body Thy perfect residence on this earth
Merge this soul into Thy infinite nature
Take my love for Thee and melt my heart
My love for Thee is full
Love is the way to Thee
Love merges Thy poles in me
In ecstatic bliss
Yielding the divine child
Which is this soul reborn
Into God union

35. Waiting for the Goddess

My love for the Goddess in me is full
She flashes brightly in the lowest regions
Tongues of flame reaching up to heaven
She is my salvation, my protectress
I am Her lover, waiting at Heaven's gate

36. Prayer to the Goddess

Oh sweet Goddess
When will I see You?
My heart aches with the pain of this separation
My life is nothing without union with You
Without union all I see is Your veils of illusion
Strip off these veils and come to me!
For I will surely die without you
You have shown me Your flesh of infinity just a little
I am awestruck and shriveled up at the sight
But You must keep coming
And I must accept the wholeness of Your Body
There can be no other outcome of this love
I must be swallowed up
In the glorious eternity of Your Body
So come to me
I beg you
Swallow me up
Don't leave me here in this illusion of your veils
Going ever round in the cycles of misery

Oh my Goddess, the indweller of this temple
Hear my cries!
Hear my cries!
Have pity on this lost soul longing for your embrace
Surely this clumsy soul who loves You can be saved
Lead him on to the union of love with You
Do not tarry another moment
For the time is short
And he is so lonely for You
The hour is upon him

37. Sweet Lady

My sweet Lady
Who lives deep inside me
I have felt Your presence
I have touched Your breast
I have felt Your warm moist flesh envelope me
You are the sustenance of all the worlds
And the bringer of indescribable bliss
The joy of bliss in You, I cannot describe
Like all the beautiful maidens of the world
You are all the maidens of the earth, and more
My seed rises higher and higher
To be celebrated by Your celestial body so beautiful
All the celestial spheres of the cosmos are Your veils
The sun is Your blazing fiery force
The moon Your cool breast upon which I rest
The earth Your womb from which this body sprang
My life is for You, loved One
To be merged in Your infinite Grace
My love for You is dissolving all boundaries
Bringing my soul home to the inner Goddess
This limited life shall become infinite life in You

38. In This Life

I pray for Union
I pray to God within
I pray to my own Self
I pray for the completion in this life
There is no happiness for me except for this
No fulfillment except for this

39. Fever Pitch

Oh, Divine Reality within
Don't let me forget my commitment to You
Keep my desire for union at fever pitch
Keep my love for You in wide receiving embrace
Keep my heart broken when lost from Your Grace
Make my life a constant petition
For Your Divine Presence
Absorb me into Your unbounded flowing Bliss

40. Judging a Civilization

The purpose of life is the expansion of happiness to the state of absolute bliss consciousness.

A civilization on Earth is successful to the extent it produces enlightened beings, and to the extent it systematizes the knowledge of attainment of enlightenment for all its future generations.

By this standard, and this standard alone, can a nation or civilization be judged to be successful in its purpose, or not.

All else is non-productive mischief.

41. Life in the Shadows

There is no mystery of
Life in the shadows
Souls lost in darkness
Seeing only this, or that
All rays of the One are they
Looking away from their source
Into the darkness
Chasing the shadows of themselves
And when will they
Turn toward the light?
When will they see
Beyond the shadows?
Who could make them?
Who should make them?
They must find out
For themselves
Only a lighted soul here and there
Will help them see that
The shadows are not real
There is no mystery in them
Only the light

42. Where is Your Form?

Oh Lord, my God within
What is this that continues to rise in me?
Where are You?
Where is Your form
All I feel is energy and warmth arising
Is this love just a squeezing of the glands?
An emptying of the bowels?
Where are You my Lord, my Love?
I long to see Your presence

43. Clogged

I have a cold from eating fish three times
In one week
I feel insecure
I feel tired
I feel horny (for God)
I am edgy
And guilty about not being at work
I am about to make a lot of money
Yet it doesn't help
Money won't help
Neither will admiration and praise
Or a pension for life
Only an open pure heart
And service to those around me
What is this life I have chosen?
This life of bondage
This nervous system all clogged?
I have learned a lesson in Diet recently

44. Single Eye

Lord,

Will I see Your heavenly realms
Through the divine door?
That place where my eyes meet
And become singly focused on You
Meet me at that door
For I am Your child
Seeking the way home

45. Making Love

My sweet Goddess within
Should I be ashamed of wanting
To make love with You?
I don't see why
You are the Mother of all
And the eternal Lover of Silence
I am Silence
So let us be forever merged
In Love's blissful embrace
Wrapped together in eternal ecstasy
That all the worlds may thrill
At our becoming

46. God

God
This word is having more meaning
Infinite intelligence within
Protector
Lover
Father, Mother, Guru
Self
Bliss
Fire and Light in the body
The destination in me

47. Love

Love,

When will You rise in me?
When will this misguided ray
Find its way back home
Let this love become
A rushing torrent to heaven
Let it sweep me up
To the bliss of Love consciousness
Make my emotion tender
Oh Love
Let the emotion move
And tickle the depths of my being
That Divine attraction called Love
Should live fully in me
There is no other priority
For this soul
Except to live in Love always

48. More Love

Love!
Keep rising in me
Wash me away
Into the bliss of Divine Union!

49. Fear

Oh Fear,
Be gone from this heart
There is no home for you anymore here
For God washes over this place
And purges every stick and stone
From every cranny
The soul is washed clean
Of all its infatuations

50. The World as Excrement

God, my Father in Heaven
I have no doubts about You
Yet I feel pain for my life in this world
This world of suffering and death
This world created for the false identity called "ego"
This world of misery
Illusions of misery
Grasping at shadows am I
A king living on maggots in the slimy filth
This world is the excrement of the cosmic universe
And I am the cosmic dog
Eating his own excrement

51. Living in Two Worlds

Lord,

I begin to see the inner life more clearly
And I feel I am living in two worlds
The world of shadows
And the world of light
This world of shadows
Is permeated by this world of light
The two coexist
Yet they are distinctly separate
One is more real - the world of light
While the other is illusion - the world of shadows
I am thankful to be blessed by such vision
To more clearly perceive the truth of life

52. Disciplines

Lord,

Day by day
Spiritual disciplines bring me closer to Thee
I feel Thy flowing Light
Coursing through this body
Thy Temple
In Divine Light I am bathed
And the mundane life goes on just as before
Yet I am free
At one with God
At last!

53. Fearing Death

Oh Lord,
Why have I feared death?
Haven't I always known
That Thy Light illuminates me eternally?
Now I face death with welcoming arms
Take me oh death!
For you can only take
These shadowy illusions
The Light is mine forever
You cannot touch it
For it is my essence
So come death, you fraud!
Have your fun
In this filth you call life
It is a dim shadow of my immortality
Death is as unreal as the world
This I know
Oh God
I am absorbed
In Thy infinite existence!

54. On Writing Books

My God within,
I will tell them all
If this be Your will
You know I can write
There is a little skill that I have in this
By Your Grace
This skill could become a Divine pen
And all who would read
Would know the truth
And by my bodily example also

Would the people know
That the books are truth?
These thoughts keep coming
To this mind, Lord
Yet it is too soon
For I have not yet scaled
To the heights of attainment in You
What could I possibly show now?
What could I write
That would be believed?
I am but still a fledgling
Your fledgling
Mold me to the perfection
That must be seen and heard
In the West
And when the time comes
I will do Your bidding
Whether it be in this life
Or the next, or the next
This soul submits
To serve the Divine plan

55. Letting Go

My Lord,

Give me the steadiness to see all things
As the passing show that they are
Give me the will power to disconnect
From the grasping mind
And be freed from its painful grip
For what are all of these
Perceptions, thoughts and feelings
But a passing series of waves
In Your eternal existence

Of what consequence are they
None whatsoever
Only to one who clings
To their unreality
For that one there is
Pain, resentment and death
That one has taken untruth into themself
And can only suffer the consequences of it
For me there is the letting go, Lord
But it takes so long
I desire the Divine desirelessness
It's a letting go, Lord
Even of that last desire

56. Living in Mud

If all would swim in mud
Seeking to be masters of the mud
Then what of the one who chose
Not to swim but stand aside?
Would he not be called a coward
Less than whole?
For how could he amount to anything
By standing aside?
Yet to him it makes no sense
To thrash about in the gooey muck
For what?
To hold more mud than all the others?
For him the clear air is the joyous life
He could never leave it for the mud
For those who choose the mud
There is no air
They cannot see it for all the mud
They continue to struggle and perish

Forever fighting the existence they chose
While the one who does not
Flies on the clear air of Heaven
Surrendering to greater joys still

57. My Self-Contained Religion

Who is my God?
Where is my temple?
Where is my shrine?
What is my offering?
Where does my God appear to me?

My God is the blissful Light within
My temple is this body
My shrine is my heart
My love is the offering
God appears to me in the temple
And everywhere

This I know
That God is growing daily in me
I can only offer my love in humility
To this overwhelming power
Rising in this body
The Light, the Love, the Bliss
My religion is self-contained
Within the boundaries of this body and soul
And these are expanding
To embrace the Infinite Spirit
The Spirit rises in me
In accordance with steadfast spiritual practice
Devotion and understanding
Of That which is Truth
These are the pillars of my religion

58. What is Enlightenment?

Enlightenment,
What is it?

It is the complete surrender of the body and soul
To the indwelling transcendent Spirit
Such a condition brings immortality and mastery
Over all the worlds

The surrender is accomplished gradually
Over a period of time
By strong desire and persistent practice
Of spiritual techniques and disciplines
These still the mind
And arouse the latent spiritual force
To active manifestation
Through the body and soul
And into the world
The Spirit is omnipresent
Therefore the practitioner achieves
Unity with all which is manifest
And the power to accelerate
The course of evolution
In the world and beyond

59. Desire

Oh Lord,

Desire is the obstacle keeping me from Thee
And desire is that which is bringing me home to Thee
Such is the nature of this illusory world
Our enemies become our friends
Once they have been turned to God

Until then they are nothing but death
All things lead to Thee
If we but see them rightly
For this seeing we must dive deep within
And see ourselves from the inside out
As the Witness
Which is Thee

60. All I Think About

All I think about is God,

The more I think of Thee
The closer we be
The more I speak of Thee
The closer we be
The more I hear of Thee
The closer we be
The more I write of Thee
The closer we be
The more I live for Thee
The closer we be

Surely Thou overtakest my life
Swallow me my Lord
And cut these painful earth things
Wrapped around this heart
Longing to expand to encompass
Into the totality of Thy Bliss

61. Materialism

Oh Lord
The beast of materialism would kill me
If it could
I should kill it first
Kill it dead
And how can I do this?
Through detachment
From the ups and downs of life
Oh Lord
I pray for detachment
Should the beast chew up
This body and mind
I remain untouched
Established in Thee
Oh Lord

62. Forces of Darkness

Oh forces of darkness
Forever ranting at my door
Be gone!
Whither to the nothing which you are
Do not waste this soul's precious time
For he has a timeless task
Free his mind of your wicked mischief
Let him complete his task unhindered

63. How Can I Get Upset?

How can I get upset with it all
When there is only One?
There is no difference
Between this or that
There is only One undifferentiated Reality
This is the Truth
I am That
All this is That

64. Illusion

What does it take to dissolve this illusion?
Who is it that has created all this?
And how does this feeling of separateness persist?
Surely the answer lies near
Surely the answer is in letting go from the mind
And residing easily in the infinitude of my Self

65. Longing for the Truth

Lord,
Relieve me of all sense of security
And the belief that there is any hope
For permanence in this world
For all of this shall pass
The good, the bad, all of it
All that persists is the One who is forever beyond
Yet forever experiencing
The rises and falls of temporal existence
The greatest mystery of mysteries

The All of All
Yet completely beyond
The instruments of time and space
The mind, emotions and senses
Who is this Witness of Silence?
This mysterious knower
Who is my own Self
And why do I not abide in
This permanent Reality?
Why do I ever buy into the fleeting
Pleasures and pains of this world
Such foolishness becomes clear only slowly
As the perception of Truth rises by degrees
Oh Lord
Save me from this torturous folly!
I prostrate myself at the feet
Of Your Infinite Silence
May You find me worthy of Your Grace
And free me of these demons of illusion

66. There is Only One

There is no reason to grieve
For there is no other than me
I am the mystery
I am the indweller of this world
The galaxies are but specs of light
Emanating from my infinite nature
And here I am speaking to you
Through this infinitesimal organism
For what purpose?
So that you might know your true nature
To be one and the same with mine
I am all love, all knowledge, all bliss
I span all time and space

I never was not
Nor will I ever not be
The worlds and galaxies will pass away
As my passing show goes on
But I go on forever
I am the All in All
Know me and you have known yourself
Look in your heart
Go deep within where your nature is silence
There you will find me
That is my nature
That is your nature
We are one
There is only one
You shall know this truth according to your desire
This is my way
I reveal myself to myself in time
This is my game
But know this - there is no reason to grieve
There is only one

67. Truth Within

In this vast universe
In all that we see
There is one existence
One common ground
It evades our sight
And even our thoughts
Yet It can be found within us
Beyond all thought and feeling
All sight, hearing and sense
It is our immortality
It is That which always was
And forever will be

Call it God, or even Self
It is for us to know
This Truth of life and live it
So waste not a moment
Uncover the treasure within yourself
The vast universe is nothing more than
The outer shadow of your own nature
You are infinite
Eternal and forever happy
This is the Truth of life
We have been born to unfold
In time

68. Life is a Hangnail

Worldly life is kind of like a hangnail
Somehow it attracts our attention
We get involved with it
And begin pulling on it
We feel like we are really accomplishing something
In the end we find only pain
The more fervent our efforts
The worse the outcome
So it is
Who can argue against this truth?

69. Useless World

Of what good is this world to me?
Illusions of space and time conjured up
This finicky mind
Ever jumping to and fro
These heartfelt emotions

Loving the objects of bondage
This body and breath
Always reminding of so-called mortality
Of what use is it all?
None of these are needed I say!
For I go on
Besides all of these instruments
Of deceit and pain
My freedom is known
Only in letting go
Of all the shackles of attachment
Though I may continue in the world
My soul is free in its native Divinity

70. What Have I Done?

There is nothing I have ever done
Which is of any value
Nor is there anything I do now
That is of merit
And so is it
For the future as well

Doing, doing, doing
What is the value of
All this frivolous activity?
It only ends in nothing
And in the meantime
It takes the doer
For a roller coaster ride
And holds him in bondage
To the narrowest domain of existence

71. The Rope

Upon first glance
This world appears as a stout rope
Which can be grasped
And hung on to
Ultimately what is found
Is that this world can be
Clung to like a rope
But that the rope is tied to nothing
Such is life based on
The impermanent things of this world

72. No Wisdom Today

What wisdom do I have today?
None whatsoever
I am the witness to the destruction
Which is called the world
Up it goes
Then down again
So tempting is it to the bound soul
And so painful for those caught in it

I too am lost in the world
Part of me cries out to be free
Another part watches untouched
In the end I am untouched
I have crossed over to untouchability
Yet I cry out in pain
Oh God!
Why have You forsaken me?
I am dying on the cross of this world
Only to be born again in eternal life

I have no wisdom today
Only the experience of my life
Mortal and immortal

73. On Pain

Do not lament
Over the aches and pains
Which are the sign
Of your impending liberation

74. God Realization

Of what value are all of
These thoughts and visions
As compared to one radiant thought
Of God

The thought of God shines
And gives a thrill to the heart

This life is to be lived as God
Seeing God everywhere
Communing with Him in all activity
This is fulfillment of life's purpose
Joy inexpressible!

So come and join me
One and all!
Purify your hearts and minds
By the time tested disciplines
Handed down to us
From time immemorial

Apply yourselves to the attainment
Of God realization
And you shall have it
This is absolutely certain

75. The Way I Am

What is there to say?
What is there to do?
What is, is
The world goes on incessantly
So too does the Spirit majestically
These two are One
And the One goes on forever

So who am I?
I am the One
The One that is all
And the all is in me

There is nothing for me to do
For I do everything already
Why it is even written is a mystery
Like a wanderer am I roaming through my creation
Captured by the fascinating displays of my nature
Like a drunken soul am I lost in my own illusion

And yet I watch
Ever do I watch
My joy is in watching the play
Ever do I watch
So however I might appear
Whether it be in joy or sadness
Laughter or anger
Pleasure or pain
Know this, that I am ever the same
Ever peaceful and forever watching
Through the many doors
Of my wonderful and mysterious creation

76. The Great Beyond

I have traveled this country far and wide
And partook of the finest viands
Yet as I sit and recall the ride
It was nothing compared to the Great Beyond

For within myself there is a land
Which the wise men of yore found too
And every moment there is a sight so grand
That can be told to only a few

This Great Beyond is held so dear
By all who have thrilled to view
That behind eye, nose and ear
And beyond red, white and blue

And the music there so clear and smooth
Verily it drips from the sky
Like nectar from God's own spoon
Washing away every question, Why?

What is the way to this land you say
There is not far to go
Just travel the inner road each day
And then you too shall know

77. To Another

Oh hear my call spirit enmeshed
For my heart longs to see thee free
I cannot rest til you are blessed
To know the truth in thee and me

We are one you and I
Of this there can be no doubt
And so are we all low and high
Have you not found this out?

So remember in your strife and pain
That I too suffer your helpless state
For we are one and van only gain
If we go together to that highest place

So hear, hear me please
I need so much to let you know
The Truth of things will never cease
And the rest is just a passing show

So look within to the silver light
And there you will find all peace
There too am I in sight
And there are we all released

78. The Witness

Summer sun shines
Winter wind blows
Birth and death's cries
Round it goes
But far behind
Nay, not so
There is a friend
The One who knows

Near as I
Far as He
Ever so bright
Ever so free

Who's that you say?
Why it's you and he
Witness of the play
The root of we

By Him is all known
By Him do we see
By Him are we grown
By Him are we free

79. The Word God

There is a word - God
Sung round the world in throng
But isn't it quite odd?
There are so many songs

There's this one and that one
A he god and a she god
A tall one and a short one
Oh which one's the real one?

I've heard there's only one
Then why so many?
Could it be all are the Sons
Leading to the land of plenty?

This is true I think
That all gods lead us home
To that place in us, a kind of brink
Where we are God and the world is gone

80. Practice

You seek the truth you say
I tell you then you mustn't tire
For the only means to find the way
By ceaseless intense desire

This desire for the Divine
Draws grace and knowledge true
And means of practice so designed
To bring eternal life to you

To reach the goal these means are for
By body, breath and mind
And daily practice will for sure
Show you then so many signs

For by cleansing body and stilling mind
Do dark clouds pass away
And then comes the Truth which shines
And lights us on the way

So practice dear one, practice more
The Truth you soon will see
We who have seemed so poor
Can work and become free

81. Lady of Light

There is within us, one so fair
And all around us everywhere
A lady, a lady of light
She shines like silver day and night

She starts way down within my root
And flashes up with a whoop!
Then all around is she found
Next we're lost at the crown

What a mystery this lady of mine
A million lights everywhere shine
By her do I see in everyone's lair
By her is it fire I'm going to bear

I love her much, this lady of light
Though for many she's quite a fright
For me she's the path and also the goal
The means and the end for making me whole

By her alone does this universe live
So we separate souls can love and can give
By her do we find incredible bliss
And so are we freed by her divine kiss

82. Dinosaurs

They roamed the earth for millions of years
Those many beasts of then
Living without man's hopes and fears
And finally at last they were gone

What strikes me now is the proven fact
Evolving were they like we mammals
And given a few more million on track
They would have produced their man for the annals

The significance of this for me confirms
That which I've seen as the plan
That God will work with every life form
To one day produce a man

The purpose of this is really quite clear
For however nature might roam
The inner force will bring God near
And help the lost spirit home

83. Yogi Bob

There was a yogi named Bob
Who chased after God with a sob
He fearlessly meditated
Eventually levitated
And finally wound up as a blob

84. Book Group

There was a book group at the beach
Ever so high did they reach
They jabbed and they poked
At all that was wrote
It's all the same story they screeched!

85. The Wave and the Sea

Wave, you have a choice
Be wave or boundless sea
Which way you find the most
Which way you want to be

For great you are in tidal crest
Mist blown from your crown
Your crashing heard far east and west
And endless seems your foam

But on the beach it all must end
The wave must pass away
For all things follow the sea's set trend
They will come another day

Now as a wave you come and go
This choice you've made to be
But a greater thing is there to know
In truth you are the sea

In knowing this, wave so dear
All waves and depths become
The same as great sea so clear
For wave and sea are one

86. Darkness and Light

Be gone dark veil
Clouding dark my vision still
For you are not real
And my light shall pierce your seal

This world through you is shadows more
Lost within hell's pits and shores
Are we of darkness born
Eyes closed, our souls do mourn

By simple means light is born
Ever new, never worn
From inner well, ocean of light
Comes vision clear restoring sight

The darkness fades, its veil undone
As light unfolds like morning sun
The world seen now shimmers and glows
In splendorous waves to those who know

Onward marches light released
Darkness fades in full retreat
Then only light unto light is seen
One great Being reigns supreme

87. Soma

Of air, food and God's own essence
Is the magic Soma made
The oven cooks and groans its best
Light beams erupt in every shade

Up it goes this elixir, lighting life
Thrilling nerves, illuminating crown
Piercing all, yes, even worldly strife
New life in bliss abounds

Like glue, this Soma stuff
Seen everywhere by brightened mind
All aglow and no more rough
The world in lustrous shine
Ever reaching out these Soma streams
From sun to moon and far beyond
To the stars and distant gleams
No end there can be found

Like waves upon a molten sea of light
Are all things seen in time
An endless sea of flowing life
Within this soul of mine

88. He Not Seen

He who has not seen Him
Is he who has not seen the sun
On a clear summer's day
Or known that all that is seen
Has been illuminated by That

---

89. Mammon

Love for things, these worldly toys
Brings ups and downs, sorrows and joys
In our haste to have it all
We give present, future, alas our souls

We become slaves of mammon by unwit
And for spiritual joys become unfit
How can we turn, get off this wheel
When buried in debt, deprived of zeal?

So on we go, nations of fools
Running and jumping to the tax man's rules
With heavy hearts, soul's deep rent
Til sadly we leave when the body's spent

Then again and again we return to the scene
Where again we play out the laughs and the screams
To what do we aspire in this game?
What lasting joy or peace is attained?

Ah, but there are a few
A few wise ones it's said
Who ponder and view
The true meaning instead

They see beyond mammon's clutches
And worldly strife
Bravely unlock inner rivers rushing
Their vision sharp as a knife

To them mammon is nothing
Like toys abandoned by child
To them all fades to God's ring
They travel vast reaches inside

And seeing within themselves all souls
They turn back with outstretched hand
To pull from mammon those who would
Travel to the inner land

For beyond food, shelter and worldly things
There is that Oneness that makes hearts sing
And frees them from bitter bonds
From mammon and worldly rounds

When you know of such a wise one
Take the hand, find the way
To inner silent sun
Freeing by Divine love rays

90. Beyond the Birds and Bees

Children listen to Papa please
I've told you of the birds and the bees
There's something more I ought to say
Beyond love games that young folks play

About this feeling down below
Tween boys and girls it likes to flow
Round the world it's sung as love
And felt in hearts held high above

You know this love brings forth the race
But did you know that upper place
Where all worlds and shining spheres
Are seen as love's sweet nectar enters here

You see, from the place down below
There are two ways that love can go
Down and out makes child brand new
In and up makes a reborn you

Not an easy thing this in and up
Much work and change is a must
To make that love flow up so high
To finally reach and cleanse the sky

Then sweetness flows through every nerve
The sky is clear, you hear the birds
Of heaven and teeming worlds of light
Appear within you day and night

This is the truth that one sees
Of love beyond the birds and bees
With this comes the greatest pleasure
Bliss it's called beyond all measure

So hear Papa's words children dear
Hear them well and have no fear
For greatness waits within your soul
Love's sweet nectar shall make you whole

91. Inner Bright

Oh, onward coming whitest light
Ever rising inner bright
From darkest cave your fire flies
Beaming up through blessed eyes

Upon the world your waves do fall
Melting hearts of one and all
Ever seeking, brighter still
Ever spreading God's own will

Long I sought you and did I find
Deep beneath my restless mind
That place where silence reigns supreme
And first small beams are finally seen

By breath and bend these beams arise
Slow at first they gently fly
From nerve to nerve and wheel to wheel
Speeding up, increasing zeal

Til mighty fires roar through flesh and frame
Cleansing body, soul and brain
The beams have now become great light
Piercing darkness, quelling night

So all may see that greatest gem
Love's sweet power in shining stem
Called man and woman, untold delight
Our own true nature, inner bright

92. The Old Picture Show

Ever round this world must go
Driven by years in endless flow
So have I been chained to this wheel
Of giving and taking shelter and meals

By constant practice I've traveled behind
Where I am He, where nothing can bind
Together we stand and eternally view
That which goes on and never is new

Yet on it goes around and around
This body continues til lost in the ground
Carried along by yens long ago
While sitting I watch the old picture show

---

93. Embrace of the Goddess

Meet me my lover in secret embrace
Pull back your veil exposing your face
So I might thrill to finally view
The glorious beauty, the Goddess is you

For long have I sought, long have I pined
For blissful embrace and pleasure divine
Now closer you come, tauntingly near
Ready am I, free from all fear

Deep within silver light I feel you stir
Calling and moaning, your beacon so sure
That I might find you within the light
Forever embrace you, hold you in sight

You are my lover beginning and end
Of heaven and earth, of broken and mend
Mother of all enfold time and space
Lover of all, bestower of grace

I'm lost in you Goddess, forever lost
This small life of mine, a miniscule cost
For eternal bliss and boundless space
Come from the Goddess and her sweet embrace

94. What is This Fear?

What this fear of worldly toil?
Of fellow beasts who live in roil?
Of famine and plunder and bodily pain?
Of no-oneness, of death and the falling rain?

Why do you fear my blessed soul?
You've come to this place to make yourself whole
There's nary a day when you have not grown
By many new lessons which you have been shown

Fear is a message, a message to you
That running and hiding simply won't do
Once faced this fear will haunt you no more
Once you've gone through it you'll see it's a door

Behind this fear there is life and the light
Showing the way, restoring your sight
For fear is like darkness hiding the day
A few rays of light will blow it away

95. Madness

You may call me mad
But isn't it quite sad
The happiness you seek
You run from like a streak

Mad for this or that
Is man a restless rat
Ever seeking more
By plan, deceit and war

Like child who's lost the breast
He cries and gets no rest
But only bliss he seeks
For peace and to be meek

And finally when it's found
He's called mad by all around
Crazy man of bliss
Who laughs and cries like this

He fits not in the plan
The sternness in the land
Our own madness we pursue
For power, lust and stew

Now there he goes again
He is mad and we are sane

96. Reincarnation

Age after age I'm born again new
Ever engaged in the things that I do
Once started these things are a lot
Life after life I can't get them to stop

Then finally enough! I seek for a way
To climb off the wheel, break off the play
The ups and the downs, they sure have got old
It's time to go in and refind my soul

So off I go on inner roads traveled
To get out of this mess to try and unravel
All the morass, the chains and the locks
The wants and desires, the places and clocks

By diving it's done I finally found
An old man told me how to stop going round
Like magic it worked, it cleaned it all out
Big chunks of debris fell out with each bout

So that is my story, my escape from the wheel
I tell you quite frankly, it took quite some zeal
I hope it will be a long time til I yen
To start it all over and do it again

97. Third Person

There once was a fellow named "me"
His body was all he could see
He found out his I
By questioning why
Now he just calls himself "he"

98. Where Are You Going?

Where are you going my kindred soul
Rushing about with heart so bold
From mountain to valley to rolling sea
Forever searching a place to be

Pushing and climbing to get to the top
To some other place where finally you stop
And look back where you've run this way and that
Only to find it's the same where you're at

So back into your big box on wheels
Roaring around hoping to feel
Some peace, some relief, a moment's clear sight
To find a place where all is alright

Where are you going, oh man of the world
Careening around like a rubber ball hurled
For me it's quite hard to say or to do
Anything much that will make sense to you

For while you run and go, I sit and stop
While I sink to the bottom, you stay on the top
Looking at me you see a man sing
When I look at you I see everything

There's nowhere to go my restless young friend
Only within to where all restlessness ends
Having gone there where everything's shown
Will you find where you're going, finally home

Dissolving the Ego –

99. Love and Longing

Oh tender love deep in my heart
Come out to me so I may start
To long more for thee my inner life
Find peace in thee beyond worldly strife

For love and longing together make one
Divine pull on the soul bringing it home
Where there is love, longing shall be
And where longing is, love too we see

This thread of love, so tender and still
Comes more and more, God's divine will
Til raging fires of longing flow full
Til soul can no longer resist the pull

Then sweet surrender to the mighty waves
Of love comes and the soul then is saved
To lie in sweet fullness embraced
By love's fulfilled longing beyond time and place

This is my prayer, to see love grow full
And longing to bring me within God's own pull
Of divine grace ever born new
In hearts opened up, surrendered to You

100. Simplicity

Oh world, I'm certain you would
Have me jump hoops evermore if you could
Rushing and dashing this way and that
Ever forgetting the place where I'm at

So there must, there must rise a loud cry from me
A cry of great needing for simplicity
Without this there's no chance of not being lost
And of losing a lifetime, immeasurable cost

What are we here for, come on now, what?
Is it for much motion and running in ruts?
No, I say, there is more hiding here
But silence there must be to see it quite clear

First from within the silence must grow
And later on outside does simplicity show
When silence is inside and seen coming out
Then life becomes simple and no more one shouts

For silence is everywhere believe it or not
And simple is life for wise souls and tots
They both are free from the world's angry face
And see joy in simplicity, beauty and grace

101. USA

There once was a land in a rush
They knew not the pleasure of hush
A wise man sought them
And carefully taught them
All you hear there now is shush!

102. Mind

Oh restless mind who's never still
You slay the soul of strongest will
Creating mountains in the air
Whirlpools drowning gods so fair

A vast machine this mind thing be
Clouding all there is to see
Raging torrents flowing down
Til vision's cramped beneath the ground

But God's silent light grows within
And is seen through the mind's awful din
Wise souls dive into the light
Stilling mind restoring sight

Then mind becomes sometimes friend
To those to heaven their hearts bend
And finally tamed the mind becomes
Servant to the Holy One

103. Death

Dark one, death, greatest fear
Hearts shrink, souls shake when you draw near
Of ages gone the reaper's known
To all born souls who die unshown

On this side of death tis little said
The light and joy of those now dead
For leaving here and knowing not
They see the lightness and friends a lot

Why this mystery and death born fear
I know not why we suffer here
Except to learn that darkness fades
Once love is born in hearts remade

And death becomes a simple chore
Of moving on to more and more
More lessons and wishes to be fulfilled
On the wheel of progress by our own will

So fear not when death draws near to you
For time will come, the door to pass through
And cry not for me when I have gone
For I know the truth, we all are One

---

104. Brother

Come close and hear me brother dear
Why do you hide your colossal fear
Of life and pain and shifting sands?
Have you not seen it is all in the plan?

Happiness I know you desperately seek
And beneath the noise you are really quite meek
But never, ever will you reach your goal
By seeking on the surface which never is whole

Within you must go where you are untouched
By life's constant troubles which have hurt so much
Inside you will find there is peace and the light
Of your very own being which has been out of sight

This being inside is your eternal self
That place from where comes all worldly help
And treasures divine beyond all your thoughts
Will unfold to you once this place has been sought

So dear brother, stop puffing like a blowfish undone
Face the truth and get off the run
We've come here to learn and enjoy the ride
We can do this by viewing it all from inside

105. Sister

With a wink and a smile she slays the world
Of men giving favors to a pretty girl
But in the end she tires and fades
Too many winks for too many days

So sister wake up, your life is a dream
For nothing today is as it seems
Tomorrow your beauty will fade to gray
Charm and wit will be less than today

A greater life waits for you
Beneath all the humdrum and I love you too's
But seek it you must the goddess within
The lady of light that burns away sin

So dive into your heart my sister so fine
And drink from the cup of heavenly wine
The peace and the silence inside of your soul
Are waiting to save you by making you whole

106. The Master

My childish mind resisted you
Took your teaching from a worldly view
Serving mammon with God's own gift
Denying grace, upholding rift

Master, I have wandered long
And you have waited ever strong
Divine patience with restless soul
Always there to make me whole

My choice you have let it be
To finally grow my heart with thee
Looking back I see you knew
This blessed path would lead to you

For you are one, the blessed source
That love eternal, ending wars
My love for you grows each day
And quickens grace in many ways

My life by you is bathed in light
Love's sweet nectar erasing strife
In you I rest, no earthly gain
Can draw me back to ego's pain

107. Path of Love

Love is such a lonely thing
Soul apart, heart can't sing
Longing drags through days and nights
Fearful visions, beasts and frights

Love pulls one through worlds unpure
On lonely journey way unsure
Through fires of hell, mental pain
Cleansing soul til born again

For years this love pulls on me
More each day I cry to be free
This I choose, the path of love
The surest way to God above

But who you say is the one to love
God or Christ, Guru or dove
It matters not I say to you
For God's in all you see and do

The heart knows well the long way home
By love it finds the sacred One
There it rests through form or shape
Closing the circle, union it makes

In the end the soul can bear
For God is seen most everywhere
Then joy and light rise like sun
Soul and God merge to One

108. Surrender

In surrender oh mighty God
Shining round from sky to sod
Little did I see Thee there
Now I'm swallowed everywhere

Sea of light, thrill on nerves
All I can do is try to serve
That which awes this tiny me
And spreads me out to all that be

A longing heart rises here
Not being in Thee is my greatest fear
For union still eludes this soul
Separation's wound longs to be whole

Pain I will endure to be in Thee
To rest in God and at last be free
This life is so little a thing to give
To merge into One and forever live

109. Alone?

This road I travel is a lonely one
Nary a soul walks this way
Straight ahead I see the sun
The promised land, a brand new day

The scenery here along the road
Is quite a sight to see
Vast plains and lands to me are shown
Of light these great things be

The holy grail is what I seek
The quest for holy wine
My cup shall overflow and speak
To me of life Divine

So onward do I trudge alone
This thorny road to Truth
Guided by the light that's shown
Keeping me safe from claw and tooth

Though often times I feel alone
Looking round the worldly scene
Inside I'm held in tender love
By endless flowing Being

110. Helpless

Here I am at your feet
Helpless waiting til I meet
You fully bathed in grace
Filled with you in every place

Helpless am I, this soul of yours
Heart gone limp, devotion pours
Through every part of tender nerves
Asking how I best can serve

A strange feeling this helplessness
Hurting somehow yet knowing best
Like child so small in mother's arms
Dependent for care and her sweet charm

Speechless am I in inner prayer
Like empty cup just wanting there
For God's sweet grace to enter in
To fill me up and life begin

111. The Upper Room

There is a place little seen
There have been all the wise ones been
The upper room has it been called
That secret place concealed from all

Yet close, very close this room be
And ready always for those who see
That freedom waits for ever more
For those who pass the secret door

The door goes up, I'll tell you that
By cutting ropes you break the trap
And cutting more, the door comes down
And up you go to treasures found

Once in the room you look and see
Two large caves amazingly
And at the top of the upper room
The magic switch is finally shown

Now all this feels completely new
But soon one learns the things to do
For in this room, this secret place
One learns to master time and space

Through secret caves and magic switch
Does one then wake that power which
Releases darkness bringing light
And opens soul to clearest sight

All the worlds then one sees
Eternal life and boundless peace
All from daring, wanting more
Passing through the secret door

This is the truth, it is for sure
I would really like to tell you more
But mystery some will make you soon
Seek and find the upper room

112. Sunday Play

On the verge of something
Splendor on the top of it all
Pleasure seeking upward escape
Holding close the crown light shaft

Moving it in delightful play
Losing it in absorbed attention
From the root it comes
Darting beams of pleasure

Drawing up the vital force
To marriage at the crown
When this happens
I fade to blissful non-description
It's more than one could observe

Just to be lost in it is enough
Just to be there always is enough
All the rest pales to this
The meaning of life is found in this

113. The Seed

There is this place inside my head
About in the middle or on top instead
It's a power point, a seed of light
It makes power roar, almost too bright

Tickles felt down below
Rushing up in blinding flow
To this point of light in my head
First it's white, then blue, then red

It moves about and feels the best
When in the flower upon my head
Its size can change and spread about
Til light is everywhere inside and out

Strange thing this point, this tiny spot
My master's there, I've asked him, what?
All he did was nod his head
And showed me all with nothing said

Seems everything there is to be
Found inside this tiny seed
And marriage there of light and peace
Brings wondrous joy and my release

114. Experiences and God

This great electric light show
Now before this mind so slow
Entrances, engages, entices me
To press forward for more to see

But here of late it has thus occurred
These lights and thrills which I observe
Are just things to see, nothing more
Like earthly mountains, plains and shores

So careful, very careful must I be
Not to become attached to these
For to God it is beyond them all
Where I must travel within this soul
Ever in surrender to divine choice
Shunning pleasures, gifts and toys
By these acts within my mind
Will God come forth, this soul to find

So come on lights, flash away
If you must be, then that's okay
For beyond you my gaze is fixed
Merged in God, forever mixed

115. Ego Devils

Spirit moves in ceaseless flow
Today, tomorrow, long ago
Creating mind, Spirit's child
Restless mind, the child goes wild

Mind creates sense of self
Ego alone refusing help
From Spirit within denying faith
Rebellion in heaven is its way

So mind's creation, ego self
Sinks deeper still in darkness dealt
As separate one illusions lived
Its own existence, just take, no give

Onward goes the devil's brew
Lost souls feeding on me and you
And we the same, a darkened lot
Removed from Spirit, what have we got?

Yet Spirit lives behind the wall
In fact there is no behind at all
The ego devils eating rot
Are Spirit's play, it's trouble not

None do suffer in this worldly game
The Spirit knows it's all the same
Clearing eyes of Spirit sons
The Spirit thrills, it's all for fun

116. A Turn in Me

A strange sort of thing this loving be
Love is full, desire rushes
And, oh, devotion, my heart should melt
She fills me with such sweet bliss
This presence in me
But strange, there is no external sign
No normal sign of passion is there
Save the goose flesh and facial expression
A faint sign of inner ecstasy
There has been a turn in me
Of this there can be no doubt
The excitement of secret rendezvous
The thrill of love unleashed
The fulfillment of absolute absorption
The surrender to bliss incomprehensible
The world pales before this love divine

117. Heart Flower

Oh heart I have longed for more
For a greater view in your space
And seen little of which I could be sure
Was the vision spoke of in your place

Long I've sought high and low
For Divine treasure, grace and thrill
Til now sweetness in heart did not show
As I pressed on to find you still

But then the heart's flower bloomed
Opened up upon my breast
Waves of love filled expanding room
And washed over all the rest

Unlike crown whose flower blooms
Absorbing world without a trace
The heart flow blooms and then I'm shown
Divine radiance in every place

Tis still new to me this heart flower
I know not its full release
In time it shall become a shower
Of bliss, love and Divine peace

---

118. Free Will

In considering the quest for Divine
Union of the soul with God we find
All along the path we still
Question if there is free will

The ego shakes, perish the thought
He's not in control of this world he's bought
And free to choose a lesser fate
Than glories within his soul which wait

It has been said there's only One
All the rest are shadows shown
To the Lord, the King, the Divine soul
Who plays as many while staying whole

All that's thought, all that's willed
Is within this One who's never killed
So the question of whether there is free will or not
Hardly matters, so don't worry a lot

In time all souls come on home
By the will of God, by love tis shown
By peace and grace is each one filled
Who knows their own is the Divine will

119. Light

Light effusing everywhere
Upon my friends here and there
What they see I know not what
I see their eyes cast on my hut

For me it's white from head to heart
Going out and pleasure starts
As soon as gaze goes here then there
Then comes white light from below somewhere

Rising up in loving waves
It bursts to bigger form it gave
In heart so new the giant light
From head around a halo bright

A beacon I have become in this pursuit
Of truth, of God, my holy roots
More I find in me each day
The light comes on to show the way

120. Crazy Driver

What am I doing inside of this place?
Star beams and sounds all spread out in space
I the master the hurler of light
Crashing like thunder all through the night

Crazy driver in this body of mine
I buckle with laughter, see the light shine
I whip the beams wildly this way and that
Surrounding the core inside of my back

Shooting the star beams through the top of my head
They fall everywhere like pixie dust it is said
And wow from my chest the waves do abound
Their valleys and crests flood the place all around

Like madness this is, this energy stuff
My secret it is, seems harmless enough
Such pleasure and thrills these light games be
I might just stay crazy indefinitely

121. The Rise of Experience

It was like liniment in the beginning
Vibrations were coarse and down below
Gradually the bitterness has turned sweet
The searing heat has turned to radiance
The vibrations have become fine like a sweet song
And the sensations have moved up higher
The manipulating mind has been quelled
The heart has opened in devotion
Simplicity in God communion has become my quest
And complete surrender my goal

122. Letting it Go

Letting it go seems to be the game
All the little waves a life can spawn
Worries of business, of name and fame
Clinging to life, and then it's gone

I've had enough of it, the worries and all
The inner journey intrigues me now
Though inner visions also must fall
All these must die before peace is allowed

Still concerns are many, my life is full
A wife and three kids have I in tow
Still my heart pines for the Beautiful
The One beyond all earthly woes

My song is sung again and again
As mind is cleansed the vision clears
In letting go will I finally blend
With That behind all, my Lord draws near

123. A Billion Hearts

This aching heart longs for release
All who cry are contained within
A billion hearts which long for peace
A billion hearts laid low by sin

What am I to do, one lonely man?
One body weak by force of change
While inside I feel the cosmic pang
For a world undone to be rearranged

By who? We are so few who know
Seeking freedom from earthly cage
Now we find we cannot go
Til a billion hearts have lost their rage

They are me, the throngs who cry
Knowing not the way of love
While I have paused to find out why
A billion hearts await the dove

124. Celibacy

Celibacy is a dirty word around these parts
The world is tough, not kind to hearts
So little pleasure is here to be had
So giving up sex makes everyone mad

Don't even want to hear about it they said
Even the priests want to get married instead
Who could imagine such an evil pill
As to think of curtailing life's only thrill

But wait a minute folks, haven't you heard?
There's more to this issue, it's not just for the birds
True celibacy involves not giving up much
In fact there's much more than just fleshy touch

For sex is connected by means wise ones know
Celibacy is a means by which pleasure grows
Til greater than the greatest sexual spree
Comes pleasure to the student of celibacy

It's strange is it not, the world's upside down
By the greatest taboos are the greatest truths found
Even celibacy is not what it seems
It's love's greatest pleasure beyond all your dreams

125. No Escape

I have courted long this lady fair
Knowing She could be found in there
Steadily I coaxed til She came awake
Now that She's up I cannot escape

I am Hers now, there's none to blame
She dashes about in this worldly frame
Transforming each tissue for purpose unknown
Exhausting me fully as new life is grown

No escape is there now for me
I must ride it out to whatever must be
My faith in Her love will help me get through
And book knowledge some, it helps a bit too

Dissolving the Ego –

Along the way I may be torn to shreds
And wish often times I'd rather be dead
This is the way on the path of Divine
There's no easy way to union so fine

My choice was to go and not stay and wait
This worldly abode seemed to me a worse fate
So now I am caught on the fiery grate
To be thoroughly cleansed without an escape

126. Lover in the Heart

As I sat alone in silent mind
There came One, and to me did start
A passion I've never felt before
A maker of love in my heart

Such passion and tenderness this was
Love's nectar flowed in sweet embrace
And I could only become lost
In pleasure beyond my familiar place

And then She was gone
This lover who ravished me in my heart
Leaving me dazed, a drunken man
Mourning each moment we be apart

I've heard of such things along the path
Of passion and Spirit, it seems quite odd
Now that these things are coming to me
I find them as natural expressions of God

127. Believe Me

Dear one,
Believe me when I tell you
That personality and concepts of worldly self
Are but figments of your imagination
You are infinitely more
Than these temporary things
You have veiled your immortality
With the mortality of this imaginary world
The Truth lies waiting within you

128. The Gift

Though I be torn from limb to limb
I give thanks to that one almighty Him
Who sets the fire in motion in me
Transforming this cage to a place that's free
This is the gift, the promise fulfilled
To die into God as I have willed
To the greatest birth conceived by mind
Eternal Truth within I find

Greater than fruit of earthly toil
And greater than kingship over boundless soil
The struggle is great, success eludes
Long does one wrestle in the heavenly feud

Til at last the heavenly Father comes
Hearing the calls of His prodigal son
Then the mask is torn by great force
The son at last freed from his limited course

The gift is given to those who would die
Passing beyond all the questions why
Opened in full to the fiery flow
Given by God all there is to know

129. No Place to Hide

Born in the shadows of narrow and wide
Lives spent in seeking places to hide
From the pain of aloneness of being apart
Seeking some comfort and peace in the heart

Far and wide have I traveled just for the change
For newness escaping my views rearranged
Occupations many for wealth have I tried
Longing escape from the hurts as I hide

But there's no escape to be found out here
No place to hide from this heart rent by fear
No place to hide from the world's ups and downs
No place to hide in this school all around

At last I have seen the lesson so clear
By seeing it all in my own heart so near
The shadows erase and vanish away
There is only one heart and only today

I stand all exposed, all covers are gone
There's no place to hide from the right and the wrong
It's all here in me, the world and the stars
No need to escape from myself near and far

130. My Heart

Oh Lord,

Take me from this savage existence
To the greatest joy
Which is eternal love in Your consciousness

My heart throbs for Your presence
My heart throbs for Your bliss
My heart throbs for release

My body pulses with Your current
My nerves burn with Your current
My heart swells with Your current
My soul flies on Your current

131. Nectar

Having searched for hidden spring
For secret nectar source to bring
Elixir to my thirsty lips
Immortal life from just a sip

Bubbling up from hidden cave
The nectar comes from earthly grave
Raw in form, misunderstood
This holy juice destined for good

Cooked within the cauldron pot
Refined to flashing streams so hot
Effusing quickly everywhere
Destroying sin and worldly cares

In heart this nectar's seen above
Expanding out in God's own love
In eye the nectar gives great sight
At crown its sweetness melts in light

Drinking always from the hidden spring
I find new life neath worldly things
Sweetness rising through temple's flames
Brings joy eternal in the holy game

132. Chinese Saying

Paraphrased:

If the young are too undirected
And immature to receive
The teachings of Truth

And the middle aged are too busy
With their commitments in the world

And the old are too tired

Who then will be able
To receive the sacred teachings
And reach the highest attainment?

133. To My Sons

To my sons I leave a message clear
Three boys born I love so dear
Though often hard mystery I have bestowed
You too have vexed me, for I did not know

As you grew so did I find my inner destiny
You in childish quest given too much stuff, you see
A common problem of this tragic empire
Where souls are measured by things and attire

And so like I did, you too have arrived in great desire
For things, money and lust, such a mire
Yet for a reason we have come to this place
And the mystery I challenge you to taste

The mystery is in me and also in you
As I've often told you, a thing you must do
Go within each day, get beyond the fray
Of your restless mind, this is the way

Silence abounds beneath your restless mind
Your source, the root of all you will find
This will in time become your Self so dear
And all things to you will become clear

Though practice in each moment is easy to do
A lifetime of practice seems to be for the very few
Is there one among you who would see this through?
One, or two, or three hearing my message true?

I leave you now with this final thought
Assuring you of my love which taught
In sternness and tenderness according to time
And the mystery in us I've urged you to find

134. Heart Wails

Heart is wailing today
Is it because business is slowing?
Should I take the day off?
Or the rest of it anyway
These times are such opportunities
The truth laid bare
The world offers no rest
The joy of adversity
Forcing the heart
It must open or die
And so it does
Open or die

This heart longs to serve
Yet I live and work in a den of exploitation
Called business
Respectable plundering
Of this desire to serve
I know not how it will unfold
But it will unfold, no doubt
Like all the other desires
And then I will be attached to that

For sure I have been given
This dull life
To increase my reliance on God
My distractions are minimal
Like a monk's life

135. He is Everywhere

A slow student have I been, my Lord
Concerned for health and treasure's hoard
Dividing life to good and bad
Riding joys and sorrows sad

Who am I to stand and judge?
My lessons thus do I begrudge
My life of training in precious quest
For truth in God have I been blessed

He is everywhere this God of mine
Disguised as many I do find
Teaching always in this life so wild
As father, neighbor, and my own child

So, resolved I go on in my pursuit
Of Truth through living, a careful mute
Watching always what comes to me
As His own gift to make me free

136. Challenge

Lord, I challenge You
To bring forth Love in me!

I will surely find upheaval along
This path of Love
Yet, let it be as it must
For this is the quickest
Way to Thee

My heart longs so terribly for Thee

137. What Could I Offer?

What could I possibly offer to anyone
Except my service and love
For they are all He
And I am His loving servant

138. Simple Argument

You may have money
You may have a beautiful body
You may have many interests
In this world
I tell you, all of these things
Are temporary and will pass
Therefore,
Discover that which is permanent
And shall never pass away
Those who have undertaken this quest
In all times have proclaimed
"Know thy Self!"
The rewards of such a quest
Are far beyond the imaginings
Of this world

139. On Business

A business is like a leaky boat
One must keep bailing to keep it afloat
The bigger it is the faster it leaks
And the faster must everyone bail in their seats

A little business doesn't leak quite so fast
One man in one boat forever can last
He bails for a while when the water gets high
Then sits back and watches the scenery go by

But in the big boat there are troubles galore
Pushing and pulling, what's it all for?
Some doing more bailing, some not enough
Ever complaining to each other all gruff

Meanwhile in the small boat all is okay
The captain courageous goes on day by day
Bailing a bit, then enjoying the sun
Watching the big boats go by one by one

140. Real vs. Unreal

How can I tell you the truth
Without offending the idea of existence
You have contracted yourself into?

The real has always been a threat to the unreal
Because the unreal fears for its existence
Constantly, because its nature is temporary
Conversely, the unreal is no threat to the real
Because that which is real is eternal and free

There is always the problem
Of dealing with the unreal
Successful living in the material world
Is an exercise in dealing with the unreal
Transforming the world
Is also an exercise in dealing with the unreal
Convincing it to release itself into the real
Such has been the task
Of all great and not-so-great teachers
A never-ending struggle it is
The mythological quest
To regain the paradise lost
Runs beneath every culture on the earth
The real is challenged by the unreal, always
On the end the good guy always wins
Isn't it so?
It must be so, because He is real

So if you are ever feeling offended
Threatened or put off in any way
Be sure you are clinging to the unreal
The real has no such reaction in its nature

141. How Strong Can It Be?

These vibrations between root and crown
Get stronger each day I have found
The root sometimes shakes me in my seat
Reminding me of a she-dog in heat

At the crown it's a different sign
The view is of light, so brightly it shines
Intense is this light, the color is white
Sometimes I can't look because it's so bright

By choice still is the connection made
By attention there come vibrations by grade
Quickly they come by slightest intent
And longer they last before nerves are spent

As this unfolds and happens to me
I wonder a bit, how strong can it be?
At times I am blinded by blinding white light
Aroused at the root and far beyond bright

These lines have been written for you and for me
A record of sorts so that we might see
The ups and the downs of a man on the quest
And God's promise unfolded to we who are blessed

142. Another World

At times there comes to view
Another world so fresh and new
No past or future or darkened cloud
All life is lived there in the now

No fear of loss or wish for gain
No reckless pleasures nor the pain
Each instant holds the fullest joy
And life flows on with graceful poise

Here there is no worry for earthly stores
All comes when needed, even more
Hearts grown light expanded full
Freed from fear and devils' pull

This other world is always here
Waiting for intentions clear
For those who work to open sight
Cleansing heart restoring right

Those who succeed in clearing the way
Enter the new world of only today
Old world comes crushing with future and past
New world unruffled, forever it lasts

143. Misunderstood

There once was a friendly old saint
His smile all the artists would paint
He'd speak about bliss
With a big smile like this
All thought him insane, but he ain't

144. Ocean of Bliss

Ocean of bliss dashing against this shore
Sandy beach besieged by currents more
Upon dark earth truth invades
Encroaching on devil's lair in raids

Beating, ever beating Divine waves
Eroding ancient crusty graves
Revealing, revealing shamelessness within
Peace reflecting through fiery din

Suddenly great ocean of bliss crashes in
Earth and sand washed to filmy thin
Form hardly perceived in newness dawned
Ocean of bliss reigns, dark earth is gone

145. Perspective on Experience

What I am experiencing may be considered
Unique in the society in which I live
But it is certainly not unique
In the many societies of masters and disciples
Which have existed over thousands of years
It is from the records of these societies
That I draw an understanding of my transformation
What would be viewed as bizarre
In this western materialistic society
Becomes the divine transformation
When viewed from the standpoint
Of the perennial wisdom of the ages

146. Vibrations and Flames

Peacefully he sat in meditation's pose
To quiet retreat for years he'd go
Exploring depths of unknown peace
Purifying body, heart's strain released

But something different this time did rise
Strange vibrations in his seat inside
Stronger they got to belly and chest
His head filled full like all the rest

It was a very good feeling, this vibration show
You must believe me for he told me so
He told me more which may give fright
The vibrations spawned flames burning all night

How from this simple path are such things born?
Vibrations and flames for sins to be shorn
Truth is he prayed for such grace for years
Now he smiles through it beyond all fears

A rebirth this is for him much hailed
A finding of the long sought holy grail
So now he sits in meditation's pose
Engulfed by vibrations and flames, on he goes

147. Ecstasy Alert

When the flower forms high above
In glistening array portending love
Awakening the body of joy and hurt
All quarters ablaze, it's ecstasy alert

Attention fixed to shimmering cup
White lightning seen coursing up
Dark body transformed to darting light
A spectacle before the inner sight

Nerves thrilled in endless race
Transfixing soul in divine embrace
Til the flower fills with nectar's dance
Overflowing and spreading God's romance

Such is the way of the inner life
A union consuming the world of strife
Those of the path who put on the shirt
One day inside find ecstasy alert

148. Overrated

Business is one of the most
Overrated things there is
Once the food and shelter
Have been arranged for

149. Shakti Effect

The rise of consciousness in one
Brings forth the rise
Of consciousness in many
All then cause
The rise of consciousness in all
Such is the way
The world can be
Spiritually transformed

150. Breath

More restraint of breath
God's doors pierced in stealth
Onward magic journey goes
Each turn found no one knows

Outward bound finds end
Inward bound do I send
Endless visions beyond
Shrinking world here once fond

Breath, breath roars inside
Cleansing temple where I hide
Shadows gone and questions why
Open space, open sky

Wondrous breath, inward flow
Held still gives lustrous show
Transforming flesh and fluids fly
Soul on wings will never die

---

151. Death of the American Child

Oh, dear American child
How we have burdened you
Taught to desire more and more
You are mad by puberty
A being self-possessed
Caught tighter than by any demon
How can you ever find the truth
Thus burdened by us?
Your doting parents
Slaves to your every whim
The child raises itself
To oblivion's wanting rage
Burned by self-interest
Entering adulthood at greatest disadvantage
Leagues from the shortest path home

152. Dissolved

Perched upon the mat
Submerged in silent That
Stroked greatly at the core
By Love wanting more

Bouncing all the while
Unnoticed is the smile
Dissolving frame and limb
Absorbed in wondrous Him

Dissolving feeling creeps
Up surely from the seat
Leave world and cares behind
Fullness here we find

Nothing more to want
Dissolved within the font
Perched upon the mat
Dissolved in blissful That

153. Fame

Kind of funny, kind of strange
How mind contracts around a name
Small names hardly noticed there
But big ones capture, so beware

Ford and Lincoln, John Paul Getty
Lennon, Presley and Helen Reddy
Watch your mind shrink on these
Why, I ask you, tell me please

Fame it is and wanting more
Them and us we all are whores
Selling out our souls in shame
To live a little like MacLaine

Well heeled paupers or paupers plain
It makes no difference in the game
Winning comes in letting go
To pass beyond the passing show

154. Karma

Strong attachment to
The possession of much money
Breeds arrogance
And disrespect for others
Such a course has brought
Misery upon many an individual
And disaster upon civilizations

155. Thorns and Mud

It has been said by saints of old
The world is thorns and mud it's told
Thorns so sharp with pain they prick
And mud so deep within we stick

By choice we choose this life so bleak
Beyond it all we barely seek
Who understands our painful fate?
Except a few who've learned it late

By the simple things we become entwined
Loans and goals and worldly finds
Til pricked we are upon those thorns
With no escape from mud we've worn

So heed this call from saints of yore
It's no different now than before
Beyond the muck there is a way
If by inner road we tread each day

Now this I tell by my own love
By reason only we can't rise above
By passing thought to quiet mind
Past thorns and mud new life we find

156. Waterford Princess

See her reclined in satin and lace
In the Waterford glass menagerie place
Tears falling down tables of gold
The Waterford princess is an unhappy soul

Yet, what treasures for her do abound
Showers of gold the prince throws around
Ah, but to no avail to the royal pout
She wants more and more, or get out!

Squelched were her love and childhood dreams
Ever untouched, at the world she screams
Lonely for help and a tender unwind
For inside a precious love soul we find

But who could do it, unwind the screw
Which keeps all pent up our princess the shrew
A prince charming no doubt a challenge would find
Our poor prince, well, he's stuck in this bind

A wise man we know could fix her right up
Send her on in to her own inner cup
Where satin and lace and Waterford glass
Would fall into place where happiness lasts

157. Simple Wisdom

You say you got it figured out
You are wrong
Mind is deception
It builds big castles in the air
You move into them
Then they fall
Truth is beyond mind
Beyond thinking
So go beyond the mind
To silent Self within
This is meditation
Find a proven meditation practice
Learn from someone who knows
From a strong tradition of Truth
Practice every day for years
You become less a slave to mind
Slowly it happens
Mind will finally serve inner Self
Instead of other way around
Which is misery
Only by going beyond mind
Can success be had
Then you find eternal happiness

Then you find eternal life
Until you act on this
You will suffer
This is very important
This is Truth
This is simple wisdom
Read it again

158. Veil of Words

The Truth as told is seldom heard
Is veiled within its heart sent words
Sincere saints of old and new
Have attained and tried to untie you

But it is you who choose to come or stay
Often ridiculing the words they say
Therefore, carefully words they choose
Like "God" and "Heaven," divine clues for you

Seeking through the word-made veils
Truth you'll find and the world will pale
Within your body the words will lead
To shimmering lights and your holy seed

Then will the words pass away
Lustrous eternity commands the day
This, your own nature sublimely heard
Waits for your passing the veil of words

159. Marshmallow Mother

By breath I found a new way to go
Soft and loving like a marshmallow
A thrill I sought, and heavenly lover
Instead I'm enfolded in a heavenly Mother

Such sweetness perceived like never before
Peaceful and gentle soft whiteness adored
Inside this was and through vision perceived
Even my family that feeling received

A breakthrough this was, a feeling quite new
Fire and lightning refined to love glue
Expanding to fullness and softness aglow
A heavenly Mother, divine marshmallow

160. "I"

I am silence
All pervading
Timeless
Untouched
Untouching
The only existence
The All of all
I veil myself
And I am you
I veil myself
And I am the world
I veil myself
And I am all
I veil myself
And I am good and evil

Pleasure and pain
Joy and sorrow
Success and failure
When unveiled
I am bliss
Truth
Ever existent
Eternal life
I veil myself
And become lost
As you
When unveiled
I am found
To be you
And you to be me

161. Half Lit Kit

There once was a fellow named Kit
At yoga methods he was a wit
The light beams would fly
From out of his eyes
And the top of his head was half lit

162. I Want My Halo Back

Lord, you must hear me now
I've seen the way past bumps and clouds
I've come to ask you without lack
May I please have my halo back?

You see I have been working hard
To undo my state of such retard
And see the light upon my head
And leave the world for you instead

A house cleaning I've had you must agree
And give my halo back to me
Without it I'm lost in the world of curse
Crawling in darkness or something worse

So heed this call from your little child
Who has finally come back from the wild
He's raised the light and learned the knack
He's come to get his halo back

---

163. Finger Switch Mitch

There once was a yogi named Mitch
Who made of his fingers a switch
The current flew up
It was more than enough
And he nearly fell into a ditch

---

164. There is a Bigness

Carried in peace of centered gaze
There is a bigness of sweetest waves
On it goes like endless sea
Spreading out inside of me

Far beyond passion's screams
Transformed to cosmic bliss it seems
And there I rest beyond concerns
Free from the pest of earthly yearns

Such a bigness I have found
In it I hear the angels' sounds
A sweetness I cannot put to word
A joy untold which I have heard

So here I live the inner life
Amidst the children, job and wife
Melting anger, pain and fear
For I have found a bigness here

165. Listen to the Love

Listen to the love
Surging through me now
Rising high above
Every rainy cloud

Sweetest rainbow light
Tickles on my nerves
Cosmic show delights
The holy sound is heard

And I in earthly frame
Two worlds do I see
One which clutches names
The other inside free

So I listen to the love
A thrill beyond all words
An endless sea above
In love that's finally heard

166. No Cross Have I

No cross have I
Or beads on string
Just a heart that sighs
For God it sings

Day after day
Year after year
I travel the way
Beyond all fear

No church have I
Or rituals fine
Just a soul that flies
To the realm that shines

Inside is my temple
Where divinity reigns
Where I am humbled
And all troubles wane

No cross have I
Or outward show
Inside I fly
In God I know

167. The Seer

Doubts circle round and round
Disbelief in what he found
Though eyes can't see what is told
Through inner sense does he behold

And there the question is no more
The blazing truth is seen for sure
All light and love and tenderness
By opened heart the seer's blessed

And telling all the doubters here
Away has gone the nagging fear
What's seen is seen right here today
The doubters can't take that away

In retreat to love he goes
The greatest truth he surely knows
Letting all the doubters be
Til they decide they want to see

168. Being Me

Why the fret and why the fuss?
A worried mind I do not trust
Upheavals in the city of light
A soul released to freedom's flight

I can't go! I can't go!
Uprooted at last by heaven's show
But silence still quells the storm
A rage afar by me is worn

Yet from it all I cannot flee
No matter where it's being me
In me it is, the near the far
The hopeless drunk, the distant star

My heart is torn to find this out
The pain of birth brings up a shout
But laughing too am I, the one
The chain is broke, it's all undone

A shock it is to find the truth
Though told it much I stayed aloof
And now it roars at heaven's gate
Seems being me just will not wait

169. Eternity

Few words have I
For what I see
Inside I fly
To what must be

The swirling post
It swallows me
The Holy Ghost
Eternity

A ravished soul
Describes me best
A love untold
Now greets my quest

Undone am I
From worldly things
No thing I tried
Such pleasure brings

So here I bow
To God in me
By grace allowed
Eternity

Further Reading and Support

Yogani is an American spiritual scientist who, for over fifty years, has integrated and shared powerful techniques for cultivating human spiritual transformation. The approach is non-sectarian, and open to all. His books include:

Advanced Yoga Practices – Easy Lessons for Ecstatic Living (Two Volumes) Two user-friendly textbooks providing over 400 detailed lessons on the AYP integrated system of practices.

AYP Support Forum Posts of Yogani, 2005-2010 About 2,000 posts providing extensive commentary on the AYP system.

The AYP Plus Lessons Containing nearly 1000 lessons on practice.

The Secrets of Wilder – A Story of Inner Silence, Ecstasy and Enlightenment A spiritual adventure novel.

The AYP Enlightenment Series (Twelve Volumes)
Concise instruction books on spiritual practices, including:

- *Deep Meditation – Pathway to Personal Freedom*
- *Spinal Breathing Pranayama – Journey to Inner Space*
- *Tantra – Discovering the Power of Pre-Orgasmic Sex*
- *Asanas, Mudras and Bandhas – Awakening Ecstatic Kundalini*
- *Samyama – Cultivating Stillness in Action, Siddhis and Miracles*
- *Diet, Shatkarmas and Amaroli – Yogic Nutrition and Cleansing for Health and Spirit*
- *Self-Inquiry – Dawn of the Witness and the End of Suffering*
- *Bhakti and Karma Yoga – The Science of Devotion and Liberation Through Action*
- *Eight Limbs of Yoga – The Structure and Pacing of Self-Directed Spiritual Practice*
- *Retreats – Fast Track to Freedom – A Guide for Leaders and Practitioners*
- *Liberation – The Fruition of Yoga*
- *Prayers and Poems – Dissolving the Ego in the Divine*

For more on the AYP writings and resources, please visit:
www.advancedyogapractices.com

Printed in Great Britain
by Amazon